D1129666

INSTRUMENTS *in* MUSIC

WORLD MUSIC

Roger Thomas

Heinemann Library
Des Plaines, Illinois

Designed by Susan Clarke
Printed in Hong Kong

02 01 00 99 98
10 9 8 7 6 5 4 3 2 1

Library of Congress Cataloging-in-Publication Data

Thomas, Roger, 1956-
　　　World music / Roger Thomas.
　　　　　p.　　cm. — (Instruments in music)
　　　Includes bibliographical references (p.) and index.
　　　Summary: Introduces some of the instruments used in world music,
　　including the Indian sitar and tabla, Australian didgeridu and
　　bullroarer, and African kora and sansa.
　　　ISBN 1-57572-646-7 (lib. bdg.)
　　　1. Musical instruments—Juvenile literature.　2. Music—History
　　and criticism—Juvenile literature.　3. Folk music—History and
　　criticism—Juvenile literature.　[1. Musical instruments.]　I. Title.　II. Series.
　　ML460.T427　1998
　　784.16—dc21　　　　　　　　　　　　　　　　　　　　　　　　97-49502
　　　　　　　　　　　　　　　　　　　　　　　　　　　　　　　　　　　CIP
　　　　　　　　　　　　　　　　　　　　　　　　　　　　　　　AC MN

Acknowledgements
The Publishers would like to thank the following for permission to reproduce photographs:
Gareth Boden, p.26 (Royal Festival Hall Gamelan Department); Robin Broadbank, pp.5 bottom, 15; Trevor Clifford,
p.6 left (Hertfordshire County Music Service), p.6 right (Wembley Drum Center), p.12 left (El Mundo Flamenco); Liz
Eddison, pp.12 right, 16, p.14 (Hobgoblin Music); Alf Goodrich, pp.4, 5 top, 24; Chris Howes, pp.8, 9; Hutchison
Library, pp.20, 25, p.29 (Sarah Errington), p.2 (J.G. Fuller), pp.7 (Dirk R. Frans); J. Allan Cash, pp.18, 19; Panos
Pictures, p.11 (Penny Tweedie); Pictor Uniphoto, p.27; Redferns, p.21. p.13 (G. Brandon); Tony Stone, p.23 (John Elk),
p.10 (Paul Sounders); Trip, p.28 (B. Gibbs); Zefa, p.17

Cover photograph: Redferns/Mick Hutson

Our thanks to Betty Root for her comments in the preparation of this book.

Every effort has been made to contact copyright holders of any material reproduced in this book. Any omissions will
be rectified in subsequent printings if notice is given to the Publisher.

Any words appearing in bold, **like this,** are explained in the Glossary.

CONTENTS

INTRODUCTION

This book is about just a very few of the many instruments used in the music of different countries. This is sometimes called "world music."

We cannot visit every country where music is made. But we can still find out about the thousands of different instruments played across the world.

There are many kinds of instruments in this book. Often
they will work in the same way as the instruments we're
familiar with. Today, we can hear world music in
concerts and on CDs wherever we live.

INDIA:
THE SITAR AND TABLA

The sitar has many metal strings. The player plucks some of the strings with a **pick** attached to one finger and changes the notes by pressing the strings down on **frets** on the **neck** of the instrument. The other strings add to the sound. The strings buzz against a **bridge** when the instrument is played.

tabla

sitar

The sitar and tabla are important instruments in Indian music. They are often played together.

The drummer plays a lively beat on the tablas.

The tabla is a set of two drums. One plays high notes and is often made of wood. The other has a low pitch and is often made of metal. They are played with the player's hands. The player can change the notes of the low-pitched drum by pressing the **drumhead** as he plays.

NATIVE AMERICA: DRUMS

Drums of different kinds are very important in **traditional** Native American music. The shells of the drums are made of wood. The **drumheads** are made of **hide**. The drums are often decorated. Native American musicians also use rattles, flutes, and whistles.

This drum is a Native American drum.

This Native American is playing
a traditional drum.

Native American drums have a booming sound.
They are often used in **religious ceremonies** when
they are played as people sing. They are also used
when people dance. Native American instruments
play an important role in their culture.

AUSTRALIA: THE DIDGERIDOO AND STAMPING STICKS

The didgeridoo is a long wooden trumpet made from a hollow branch. It has a **mouthpiece** made from **beeswax**. The player blows into the mouthpiece so that his lips make a sound into the instrument. The didgeridoo has one main note but the player can change it slightly by blowing harder or softer. It has a deep, growling sound.

The people who invented the didgeridoo are the Australian Aborigines.

These Aboriginal Australian dancers are using stamping sticks as part of a ceremony.

Stamping sticks are long wooden sticks which are used as **percussion** instruments. They are played by stamping them on the ground.

SPAIN: THE FLAMENCO GUITAR AND CASTANETS

Flamenco is a type of **traditional** Spanish music which uses instruments, singing, and dancing. The flamenco guitar has six strings which the player strums up and down with his or her fingernails. The guitar has two scratchplates to stop the player's nails from scratching the wooden top of the guitar.

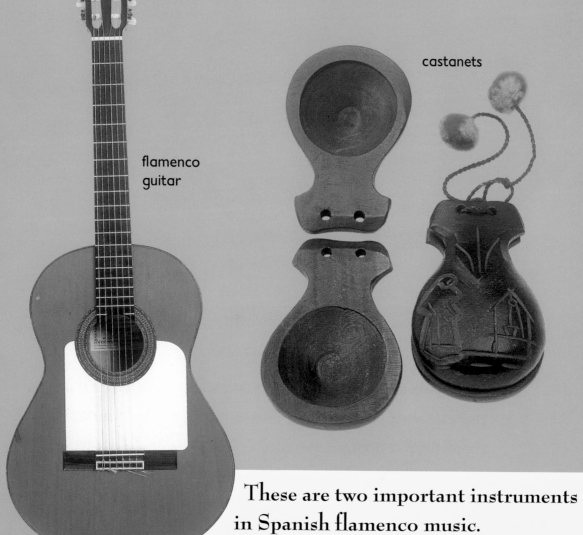

flamenco guitar

castanets

These are two important instruments in Spanish flamenco music.

Flamenco performers often dress in traditional costume.

Castanets are small wooden **percussion** instruments.
They are attached to the dancer's fingers with cords.
They make a sharp clicking sound. They are usually played
in each hand by flamenco dancers while they dance. The
dancer fits the **rhythm** of the castanets to the rhythm of
the dance.

THE MIDDLE EAST: THE OUD AND DARABOUKA

The darabouka is a funnel-shaped drum with an opening at one end. It can be made of clay, metal, or wood. The player taps the **drumhead** with his fingers to make a bright, high sound. The player can also slap the drumhead with his hand to make a deep, booming sound.

darabouka

oud

The oud and darabouka are played in many Middle Eastern countries.

This Arab musician is playing an oud.

The oud is a string instrument with a rounded back. The player plucks and strums the strings with a **pick**. The player changes the notes by pressing the strings against the **neck** of the instrument. The oud has a softer sound than a guitar because the neck has no metal **frets**.

SOUTH AMERICA: PAN-PIPES AND VIHUELA

The vihuela is like a small guitar. It was invented in Spain and is made of wood. It became used in South American music when Spanish people went to South America five hundred years ago. Sometimes in South America, an **armadillo** shell is used to make the body of the instrument instead of wood.

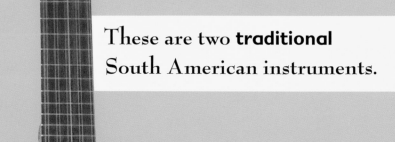

These are two **traditional** South American instruments.

pan-pipes

vihuela

This South American musician is playing the pan-pipes.

The pan-pipes are a set of wooden tubes. They are played in the Andes region of South America where they are called "yupana." They make a sound when the player blows across the ends of the tubes. The pan-pipes have a soft, breathy sound.

TRINIDAD: STEEL DRUMS

People all over the world enjoy steel drum music from Trinidad. The drums have a soft, ringing sound. Some steel drums are now made in factories but they were first made from old steel barrels. The people making them hammer dents into the top of the barrel from underneath. Then the barrel is heated to make the steel very hard.

This is how a full orchestra of steel pans is set up.

These musicians from the West Indies are playing steel drums and other **percussion** instruments.

Steel drums have different names depending on how many notes they can play and whether the notes are low or high. Some of the names are borrowed from other instruments. The names are: rhythm, ping pong, second pan, cello, guitar, and bass.

AFRICA: THE SANSA AND KORA

The sansa is made like a wooden box. A set of metal or **cane** strips is attached to the top of the box. The player plucks them with his thumbs or fingers to make the notes. Long strips make low notes and short strips make high notes. The sansa makes a sharp, twangy sound.

The sansa is played in many African countries.

The kora is played in Gambia, which is a country in Africa.

The kora has twenty-one strings and a long wooden **neck**. The neck is attached to a big hollowed-out dried vegetable called a gourd. A large hole in the gourd is covered with a tight animal skin. The player plucks the strings with his fingers and thumbs. The kora is often played when people sing. It has a soft but lively sound.

JAPAN: THE SHAKUHACHI AND KOTO

The shakuhachi is a flute made of **bamboo**. The bamboo is chosen and cut very carefully to get a good sound. The player blows across the end of the shakuhachi to make the sound and covers holes on the instrument with his fingers to change the notes. The shakuhachi has a clear, pure sound.

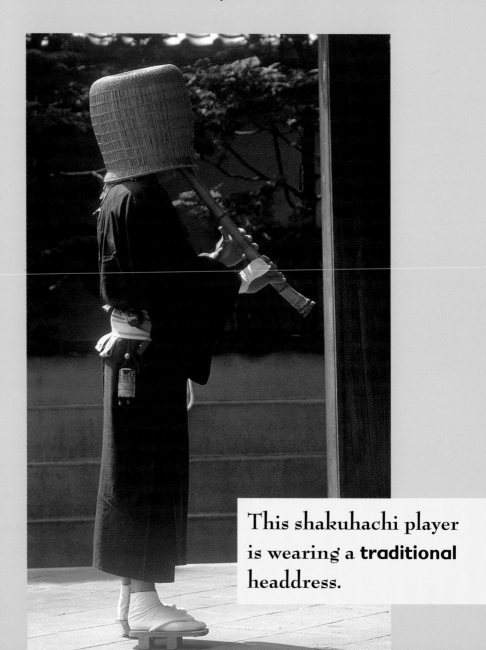

This shakuhachi player is wearing a **traditional** headdress.

These Japanese musicians are playing kotos.

The koto is a large instrument with thirteen **silk** or **nylon** strings. The player has three **picks** on the fingers of one hand and uses them to pluck the strings. Each string is stretched over a **bridge**. The player can press the strings on the other side of the bridge with the other hand while playing. This gives the notes a bendy sound.

CHINA: THE PI-PA AND SHENG

The pi-pa has been played in China for two thousand years. It is made of wood and has four **silk** strings which the player plucks. The player changes the notes by pressing the strings against wooden **frets** on the body and **neck** of the instrument. It has a soft but clear sound.

This Chinese musician is playing a pi-pa.

The sheng is a bundle of tubes with reeds inside them.

To play the sheng, the player blows into the tubes through a **mouthpiece**. To make the notes the player covers holes on the tubes with his or her fingers. This lets the air reach the **reeds** to make them sound. To stop a note, the player uncovers the hole and the air escapes before reaching the reed.

INDONESIA: THE GAMELAN ORCHESTRA

The gamelan orchestra is a mixture of **tuned percussion** instruments, drums, and **gongs**. The lead musician will sometimes play a **fiddle** or flute. There are many sizes of gamelan orchestra, made up from different numbers of these instruments.

The gamelan orchestra has many different instruments.

Playing gamelan music

The instruments of the gamelan orchestra are played with mallets. The metal instruments make a soft, bell-like sound. The drums are played with the hands and help with the **rhythm** of the music.

27

SINGING IN WORLD MUSIC

Singing is a part of nearly every kind of world music. Singers from different parts of the world use their voices in quite differently. People can sing alone or in groups.

This is a group of Indian singers.

This is a Chinese opera singer.

Singing is used in religious worship in many countries. Songs can also tell stories, give advice, or describe how the singer is feeling. Singing can also be just for fun!

GLOSSARY

armadillo   a small animal with a bony shell

bamboo   a plant which grows into strong hollow stalks

beeswax   a substance made by bees in beehives. When it is warmed it can be molded into different shapes like clay

bridge   a part of a stringed instrument with a thin edge over which the strings are stretched

cane   a piece of bamboo or a piece from a similar hard, woody plant

drumhead   the flat surface of a drum which the drummer plays on. It can be made of animal skin.

fiddle   another name for a violin. The name is sometimes used for other violin-like instruments

frets   thin metal rods on the neck of a stringed instrument which the strings are pressed against to change the notes

gongs   flat metal percussion instruments which are usually round in shape. A gong is played with a beater. It makes a note with a crashing, hissing sound

hide   dried animal skin

mouthpiece   the part of a wind instrument which the player blows into

neck   a long piece of wood on a stringed instrument which the strings are stretched along

nylon   a very strong type of plastic which can be made into strings for musical instruments

percussion   instruments which are played by tapping or hitting

pick   a flat piece of wood or plastic used for plucking the strings on a stringed instrument.

reeds   thin strips of cane or metal which make a sound when air is blown across them

religious ceremonies   special acts of worship which may involve many people

rhythm   the regular pattern of notes in music

silk   a very strong thread which is made by a kind of moth

traditional   any kind of music which has been played for a long time in the history of a country

tuned percussion   percussion instruments which can play many notes

MORE BOOKS TO READ

Hart, Avery. *Kids Make Music with Castanets.* Charlotte, VT: Williamson Publishing Co. 1994.

DeCesare, Ruth. *Myth, Music & Dance of the American Indian.* Van Nuys, CA: Alfred Publishing. 1988.

INDEX

DATE DUE

HIGHSMITH   #45102